50 Time-Saving Recipes for Home

By: Kelly Johnson

Table of Contents

- Sheet Pan Lemon Garlic Chicken
- One-Pot Beef and Vegetable Stir-Fry
- Spaghetti Aglio e Olio
- BBQ Chicken Quesadillas
- Shrimp and Broccoli Stir-Fry
- Teriyaki Salmon Bowls
- Chicken and Vegetable Skewers
- 20-Minute Taco Salad
- Pesto Pasta with Cherry Tomatoes
- Quick Chicken Fajitas
- Sausage and Peppers Sheet Pan Bake
- Mediterranean Chickpea Salad
- Easy Beef and Broccoli
- Caprese Sandwiches
- Thai Basil Chicken Stir-Fry
- Margherita Pizza
- Black Bean and Corn Quesadillas
- Lemon Herb Grilled Chicken
- Penne alla Vodka
- Teriyaki Tofu Stir-Fry
- Greek Chicken Wraps
- Garlic Butter Shrimp Pasta
- Veggie Stir-Fry with Tofu
- Avocado and Black Bean Salad
- Sweet and Sour Chicken
- Pesto Chicken Panini
- Quick Beef Burrito Bowls
- Lemon Herb Salmon
- Caprese Pasta Salad
- Chicken and Vegetable Curry
- BBQ Turkey Burgers
- Shrimp Scampi with Linguine
- Veggie and Hummus Wraps
- Spinach and Feta Stuffed Chicken Breasts
- Easy Veggie Fried Rice

- Chipotle Chicken Quesadillas
- Garlic Parmesan Zucchini Noodles
- Italian Sausage and Peppers Pasta
- Mediterranean Quinoa Salad
- Quick Margherita Flatbread
- Chicken Caesar Wraps
- Teriyaki Vegetable Stir-Fry
- Pesto Shrimp and Tomato Pasta
- BBQ Pulled Chicken Sandwiches
- Szechuan Tofu and Vegetable Stir-Fry
- Caprese Chicken Skillet
- Turkey and Avocado Wrap
- Lemon Garlic Shrimp Scampi
- Cilantro Lime Chicken Tacos
- Broccoli Cheddar Stuffed Chicken

Sheet Pan Lemon Garlic Chicken

Ingredients:

- 4 boneless, skinless chicken breasts
- Salt and black pepper to taste
- 3 tablespoons olive oil
- 4 cloves garlic, minced
- Zest of 1 lemon
- Juice of 1 lemon
- 1 teaspoon dried thyme
- 1 teaspoon dried rosemary
- 1 teaspoon dried oregano
- 1 teaspoon paprika
- 1/2 teaspoon red pepper flakes (optional, for heat)
- 1 lemon, sliced
- Fresh parsley, chopped, for garnish

Instructions:

Preheat the oven to 425°F (220°C). Line a baking sheet with parchment paper or lightly grease it.
Season the chicken breasts with salt and black pepper on both sides.
In a small bowl, whisk together olive oil, minced garlic, lemon zest, lemon juice, dried thyme, dried rosemary, dried oregano, paprika, and red pepper flakes (if using).
Place the chicken breasts on the prepared baking sheet.
Brush the chicken breasts with the lemon garlic mixture, ensuring they are well coated.
Arrange lemon slices around the chicken on the baking sheet.
Bake in the preheated oven for 20-25 minutes or until the chicken is cooked through and reaches an internal temperature of 165°F (74°C).
Optionally, broil for an additional 2-3 minutes to get a golden brown color on the chicken.
Remove from the oven, and let the chicken rest for a few minutes.
Garnish with chopped fresh parsley.
Serve the sheet pan lemon garlic chicken hot, and enjoy this simple and flavorful dish!

One-Pot Beef and Vegetable Stir-Fry

Ingredients:

- 1 lb (450g) beef sirloin or flank steak, thinly sliced
- 2 tablespoons soy sauce
- 1 tablespoon oyster sauce
- 1 tablespoon hoisin sauce
- 1 tablespoon cornstarch
- 2 tablespoons vegetable oil
- 3 cloves garlic, minced
- 1 tablespoon ginger, minced
- 1 onion, thinly sliced
- 1 bell pepper, thinly sliced (any color)
- 1 carrot, julienned
- 1 zucchini, sliced
- 1 cup broccoli florets
- 1 cup snap peas, ends trimmed
- Cooked rice or noodles for serving

Instructions:

In a bowl, mix the thinly sliced beef with soy sauce, oyster sauce, hoisin sauce, and cornstarch. Allow it to marinate for at least 15-20 minutes.
Heat 1 tablespoon of vegetable oil in a large skillet or wok over medium-high heat.
Add the marinated beef to the hot skillet and stir-fry for 2-3 minutes until it is browned and cooked through. Remove the beef from the skillet and set it aside.
In the same skillet, add another tablespoon of oil if needed. Sauté the minced garlic and ginger until fragrant.
Add the sliced onion, bell pepper, julienned carrot, zucchini, broccoli florets, and snap peas to the skillet. Stir-fry the vegetables for 4-5 minutes until they are slightly tender but still crisp.
Return the cooked beef to the skillet with the vegetables and toss everything together.
Cook for an additional 2-3 minutes, ensuring the beef and vegetables are well combined and heated through.

Adjust the seasoning if needed, adding more soy sauce or other sauces according to your taste.
Serve the one-pot beef and vegetable stir-fry over cooked rice or noodles.

This recipe is customizable, so feel free to add or substitute vegetables based on your preferences. Enjoy your delicious one-pot stir-fry!

Spaghetti Aglio e Olio

Ingredients:

- 400g (14 oz) spaghetti
- 1/2 cup extra-virgin olive oil
- 4-5 cloves garlic, thinly sliced
- 1 teaspoon red pepper flakes (adjust to taste)
- Salt, to taste
- Black pepper, freshly ground, to taste
- 1/4 cup fresh parsley, chopped
- Grated Parmesan cheese (optional)
- Lemon zest (optional)

Instructions:

Cook the spaghetti according to the package instructions in a large pot of salted boiling water. Cook until al dente. Reserve about 1 cup of pasta cooking water before draining.

While the pasta is cooking, heat the olive oil in a large skillet over medium heat. Add the sliced garlic and red pepper flakes. Sauté for about 2-3 minutes until the garlic becomes golden and fragrant. Be careful not to burn the garlic.

Reduce the heat to low to prevent the garlic from burning. If desired, add a pinch of salt and black pepper to the oil mixture.

Once the spaghetti is cooked, transfer it directly to the skillet with the garlic and oil. Toss the spaghetti in the flavored oil until it's well coated.

If the pasta seems dry, add some of the reserved pasta cooking water a little at a time until you reach the desired sauce consistency.

Stir in the chopped parsley and toss the pasta until evenly combined.

Taste and adjust the seasoning with salt, black pepper, or red pepper flakes if needed.

Serve the Spaghetti Aglio e Olio immediately, garnishing with grated Parmesan cheese and lemon zest if desired.

This dish is quick to make and relies on the quality of its ingredients, so using good-quality olive oil is key. Enjoy this flavorful and classic Italian pasta dish!

BBQ Chicken Quesadillas

Ingredients:

- 2 cups cooked and shredded chicken (rotisserie chicken works well)
- 1/2 cup barbecue sauce
- 1 cup shredded cheddar cheese
- 1 cup shredded mozzarella cheese
- 1/4 cup diced red onion
- 1/4 cup chopped fresh cilantro
- 4 large flour tortillas
- Cooking spray or a small amount of vegetable oil for cooking
- Optional: Sour cream, guacamole, salsa for serving

Instructions:

In a bowl, mix the shredded chicken with barbecue sauce until the chicken is well coated.
In a separate bowl, combine the shredded cheddar and mozzarella cheeses.
Heat a large skillet or griddle over medium heat.
Place one tortilla on the skillet and spread a portion of the barbecue chicken mixture evenly over half of the tortilla.
Sprinkle a portion of the cheese mixture over the barbecue chicken, then add some diced red onion and chopped cilantro.
Fold the empty half of the tortilla over the filling, creating a half-moon shape.
Press down gently with a spatula and cook for 2-3 minutes on each side, or until the tortilla is golden brown and the cheese is melted.
Repeat the process with the remaining tortillas and filling.
Once cooked, remove the quesadillas from the skillet and let them rest for a moment before slicing into wedges.
Serve the BBQ Chicken Quesadillas with optional sides like sour cream, guacamole, or salsa.

These quesadillas are perfect for a quick lunch, dinner, or even as a party appetizer.

Customize them by adding ingredients like diced bell peppers, black beans, or jalapeños for an extra kick. Enjoy!

Shrimp and Broccoli Stir-Fry

Ingredients:

- 1 lb (450g) large shrimp, peeled and deveined
- 4 cups broccoli florets
- 3 tablespoons soy sauce
- 2 tablespoons oyster sauce
- 1 tablespoon hoisin sauce
- 1 tablespoon rice vinegar
- 1 tablespoon cornstarch
- 2 tablespoons vegetable oil
- 3 cloves garlic, minced
- 1 teaspoon fresh ginger, grated
- Red pepper flakes (optional, for heat)
- Sesame seeds and sliced green onions for garnish (optional)
- Cooked rice for serving

Instructions:

In a bowl, mix together the soy sauce, oyster sauce, hoisin sauce, rice vinegar, and cornstarch. Set aside.
Heat 1 tablespoon of vegetable oil in a wok or large skillet over medium-high heat.
Add the shrimp to the hot oil and stir-fry for 2-3 minutes until they turn pink and opaque. Remove the shrimp from the wok and set them aside.
In the same wok, add another tablespoon of oil if needed. Stir in the minced garlic, grated ginger, and red pepper flakes (if using). Cook for about 30 seconds until fragrant.
Add the broccoli florets to the wok and stir-fry for 3-4 minutes until they are crisp-tender. You can add a splash of water to create some steam and help cook the broccoli.
Return the cooked shrimp to the wok, and pour the sauce over the shrimp and broccoli. Toss everything together to coat the shrimp and broccoli in the sauce. Cook for an additional 2-3 minutes, allowing the sauce to thicken and coat the ingredients evenly.
Taste and adjust the seasoning if needed. If you prefer a saucier dish, you can add a bit more soy sauce or water.

Serve the shrimp and broccoli stir-fry over cooked rice.
Garnish with sesame seeds and sliced green onions if desired.

Enjoy this delicious and nutritious Shrimp and Broccoli Stir-Fry as a quick and satisfying meal!

Teriyaki Salmon Bowls

Ingredients:

For the Teriyaki Sauce:

- 1/3 cup soy sauce
- 3 tablespoons mirin
- 2 tablespoons sake (or white wine)
- 2 tablespoons brown sugar
- 1 teaspoon sesame oil
- 1 teaspoon grated ginger
- 2 cloves garlic, minced

For the Salmon:

- 4 salmon fillets
- Salt and black pepper to taste
- 1 tablespoon vegetable oil

For the Bowls:

- Cooked white or brown rice
- Steamed broccoli florets
- Sliced carrots
- Sliced green onions
- Sesame seeds for garnish
- Optional: Avocado slices

Instructions:

Prepare the Teriyaki Sauce:
- In a small saucepan, combine soy sauce, mirin, sake, brown sugar, sesame oil, grated ginger, and minced garlic.
- Bring the mixture to a simmer over medium heat, stirring until the sugar dissolves.

- Reduce heat to low and simmer for about 5-7 minutes, or until the sauce thickens. Remove from heat and set aside.

Cook the Salmon:
- Season the salmon fillets with salt and black pepper.
- In a large skillet, heat vegetable oil over medium-high heat.
- Place the salmon fillets in the skillet, skin-side down, and cook for 3-4 minutes until the skin is crispy.
- Flip the salmon fillets and cook for an additional 2-3 minutes, or until the salmon is cooked to your liking.
- Pour the teriyaki sauce over the salmon in the last minute of cooking, allowing it to glaze the fillets.

Assemble the Bowls:
- In each bowl, place a serving of cooked rice.
- Top with steamed broccoli, sliced carrots, and the teriyaki-glazed salmon fillets.
- Drizzle additional teriyaki sauce over the bowls.
- Garnish with sliced green onions, sesame seeds, and optional avocado slices.

Serve:
- Serve the Teriyaki Salmon Bowls immediately, and enjoy the delicious combination of flavors and textures.

Feel free to customize the bowls with your favorite vegetables or add a sprinkle of red pepper flakes for some heat. It's a tasty and wholesome meal that's quick to prepare.

Chicken and Vegetable Skewers

Ingredients:

For the Marinade:

- 1/4 cup olive oil
- 3 tablespoons soy sauce
- 2 tablespoons honey
- 2 cloves garlic, minced
- 1 teaspoon Dijon mustard
- 1 teaspoon dried oregano
- Salt and black pepper to taste

For the Skewers:

- 1.5 lbs (about 700g) boneless, skinless chicken breasts, cut into bite-sized cubes
- Cherry tomatoes
- Bell peppers (any color), cut into chunks
- Red onion, cut into wedges
- Zucchini, sliced into rounds

Wooden or metal skewers, if using wooden, soak them in water for at least 30 minutes to prevent burning

Instructions:

    Prepare the Marinade:
- In a bowl, whisk together the olive oil, soy sauce, honey, minced garlic, Dijon mustard, dried oregano, salt, and black pepper.

    Marinate the Chicken:
- Place the chicken cubes in a Ziploc bag or shallow dish.
- Pour half of the marinade over the chicken, ensuring it is well coated.
- Reserve the remaining marinade for basting.

    Marinate the Vegetables:

- In a separate bowl, toss the cherry tomatoes, bell pepper chunks, red onion wedges, and zucchini rounds with the remaining marinade.

Skewer Assembly:
- Thread the marinated chicken and vegetables onto the skewers, alternating between chicken and veggies.

Grill or Bake:
- Preheat your grill or oven to medium-high heat.
- If grilling, cook the skewers for 10-15 minutes, turning occasionally and basting with the reserved marinade.
- If baking, place the skewers on a lined baking sheet and bake in a preheated oven at 400°F (200°C) for about 20-25 minutes, turning halfway through and basting.

Serve:
- Once the chicken is cooked through and the vegetables are tender, remove the skewers from the grill or oven.
- Serve the chicken and vegetable skewers over rice or with your favorite side dishes.

Enjoy these colorful and flavorful chicken and vegetable skewers as a tasty and healthy meal!

20-Minute Taco Salad

Ingredients:

For the Salad:

- 1 lb (450g) ground beef or ground turkey
- 1 packet taco seasoning mix
- 1 cup cherry tomatoes, halved
- 1 cup canned corn, drained
- 1 cup black beans, drained and rinsed
- 1 cup shredded lettuce
- 1 cup shredded cheddar cheese
- 1 avocado, diced
- 1/2 cup sliced black olives (optional)
- Tortilla chips for serving

For the Dressing:

- 1/2 cup sour cream
- 2 tablespoons salsa
- 1 tablespoon lime juice
- Salt and pepper to taste

Instructions:

Cook the Meat:
- In a large skillet over medium-high heat, cook the ground beef or turkey until browned and cooked through.
- Drain any excess fat if needed.
- Add the taco seasoning mix and follow the package instructions. Usually, you'll need to add water and simmer until the mixture thickens.

Prepare the Dressing:
- In a small bowl, whisk together the sour cream, salsa, lime juice, salt, and pepper. Adjust the seasoning to your liking.

Assemble the Salad:
- In a large serving bowl, arrange the shredded lettuce as the base.

- Top the lettuce with the seasoned meat, cherry tomatoes, corn, black beans, shredded cheddar cheese, diced avocado, and sliced black olives if using.

Drizzle with Dressing:
- Drizzle the sour cream dressing over the taco salad.

Serve:
- Crush some tortilla chips over the top for a crunchy texture.
- Toss the salad just before serving to mix all the flavors together.

This 20-Minute Taco Salad is not only quick and easy but also customizable. Feel free to add your favorite toppings such as diced red onions, jalapeños, or cilantro. It's a delicious and satisfying meal that's sure to please your taste buds.

Pesto Pasta with Cherry Tomatoes

Ingredients:

- 8 oz (225g) pasta (such as spaghetti or penne)
- 1 cup cherry tomatoes, halved
- 1/2 cup fresh basil leaves
- 1/3 cup grated Parmesan cheese
- 1/4 cup pine nuts, toasted
- 2 cloves garlic, peeled
- 1/2 cup extra-virgin olive oil
- Salt and black pepper to taste
- Grated Parmesan for serving (optional)

Instructions:

Cook the Pasta:
- Cook the pasta according to the package instructions in a large pot of salted boiling water until al dente.
- Reserve about 1/2 cup of pasta cooking water before draining.

Prepare the Pesto:
- In a food processor, combine the fresh basil, grated Parmesan, toasted pine nuts, and peeled garlic.
- Pulse until the ingredients are finely chopped.
- With the food processor running, gradually add the olive oil in a steady stream until a smooth pesto sauce forms.
- Season the pesto with salt and black pepper to taste.

Combine Pasta and Pesto:
- Toss the cooked pasta with the pesto sauce until well coated. If the sauce is too thick, you can add some of the reserved pasta cooking water to reach your desired consistency.

Add Cherry Tomatoes:
- Gently fold in the halved cherry tomatoes, ensuring they are evenly distributed throughout the pasta.

Serve:
- Serve the Pesto Pasta with Cherry Tomatoes immediately, garnished with additional grated Parmesan if desired.

This dish is fresh, vibrant, and perfect for a quick and satisfying meal. Feel free to customize it by adding grilled chicken, shrimp, or extra veggies for added texture and flavor. Enjoy!

Quick Chicken Fajitas

Ingredients:

For the Chicken Marinade:

- 1 lb (450g) boneless, skinless chicken breasts, thinly sliced
- 3 tablespoons olive oil
- 1 tablespoon lime juice
- 2 teaspoons chili powder
- 1 teaspoon ground cumin
- 1 teaspoon garlic powder
- 1/2 teaspoon smoked paprika
- Salt and black pepper to taste

For the Fajitas:

- 1 large onion, thinly sliced
- 1 bell pepper (any color), thinly sliced
- 1 tablespoon vegetable oil
- Flour or corn tortillas
- Optional toppings: sour cream, shredded cheese, salsa, guacamole, lime wedges, cilantro

Instructions:

Marinate the Chicken:
- In a bowl, combine olive oil, lime juice, chili powder, cumin, garlic powder, smoked paprika, salt, and black pepper.
- Add sliced chicken to the marinade, making sure the chicken is well-coated. Let it marinate for at least 15 minutes.

Cook the Chicken:
- Heat a large skillet or pan over medium-high heat.
- Add the marinated chicken slices and cook for 4-5 minutes or until cooked through and slightly browned. Stir occasionally.

Cook the Vegetables:
- In the same skillet, add 1 tablespoon of vegetable oil.
- Add sliced onion and bell pepper.

- Sauté the vegetables for 3-4 minutes or until they are tender-crisp and slightly charred.

Combine Chicken and Vegetables:
- Return the cooked chicken to the skillet with the sautéed vegetables. Toss everything together until well combined.

Warm Tortillas:
- Heat the tortillas in a dry skillet or microwave until they are warm and pliable.

Assemble Fajitas:
- Spoon the chicken and vegetable mixture onto the warmed tortillas.

Add Toppings:
- Top the fajitas with your favorite toppings, such as sour cream, shredded cheese, salsa, guacamole, lime wedges, and cilantro.

Serve:
- Serve the Quick Chicken Fajitas immediately and enjoy!

Feel free to customize these fajitas by adding your favorite toppings or adjusting the level of spiciness in the marinade. It's a versatile and delicious meal that's sure to be a hit.

Sausage and Peppers Sheet Pan Bake

Ingredients:

- 1.5 lbs (about 680g) Italian sausage links (sweet or spicy, based on preference)
- 2 bell peppers, thinly sliced (any color)
- 1 large onion, thinly sliced
- 2 tablespoons olive oil
- 1 teaspoon dried oregano
- 1 teaspoon dried basil
- 1 teaspoon garlic powder
- 1/2 teaspoon red pepper flakes (optional, for heat)
- Salt and black pepper to taste
- Fresh parsley, chopped, for garnish (optional)
- Crusty bread or rolls for serving (optional)

Instructions:

Preheat the Oven:
- Preheat your oven to 400°F (200°C).

Prepare the Sheet Pan:
- Line a large sheet pan with parchment paper or lightly grease it with cooking spray.

Arrange Sausage and Vegetables:
- Place the Italian sausage links, sliced bell peppers, and sliced onions on the sheet pan.

Drizzle with Olive Oil and Season:
- Drizzle the olive oil over the sausage and vegetables.
- Sprinkle dried oregano, dried basil, garlic powder, red pepper flakes (if using), salt, and black pepper evenly over the ingredients.

Toss to Coat:
- Toss the sausage and vegetables on the sheet pan to ensure they are evenly coated with olive oil and seasonings.

Bake in the Oven:
- Bake in the preheated oven for 25-30 minutes or until the sausage is cooked through, and the vegetables are tender, stirring once halfway through.

Garnish and Serve:

- Remove from the oven, and if desired, sprinkle with fresh chopped parsley for a burst of freshness.

Serve with Crusty Bread (Optional):
- Serve the sausage and peppers on its own or with crusty bread or rolls for a complete meal.

This sheet pan bake is not only delicious and easy to make but also versatile. Feel free to customize it by adding other favorite vegetables or adjusting the seasonings according to your taste. Enjoy your Sausage and Peppers Sheet Pan Bake!

Mediterranean Chickpea Salad

Ingredients:

For the Salad:

- 2 cans (15 oz each) chickpeas, drained and rinsed
- 1 cucumber, diced
- 1 cup cherry tomatoes, halved
- 1 red bell pepper, diced
- 1/2 red onion, finely chopped
- 1/2 cup Kalamata olives, sliced
- 1/2 cup feta cheese, crumbled
- 1/4 cup fresh parsley, chopped

For the Dressing:

- 1/4 cup extra-virgin olive oil
- 2 tablespoons red wine vinegar
- 1 teaspoon dried oregano
- 1 clove garlic, minced
- Salt and black pepper to taste

Instructions:

Prepare the Chickpeas:
- Rinse and drain the chickpeas thoroughly.

Assemble the Salad:
- In a large salad bowl, combine the chickpeas, diced cucumber, cherry tomatoes, red bell pepper, chopped red onion, sliced Kalamata olives, crumbled feta cheese, and chopped fresh parsley.

Prepare the Dressing:
- In a small bowl, whisk together the extra-virgin olive oil, red wine vinegar, dried oregano, minced garlic, salt, and black pepper.

Dress the Salad:
- Pour the dressing over the chickpea and vegetable mixture.

Toss to Combine:

- Gently toss all the ingredients together until everything is well coated in the dressing.

Chill (Optional):
- Refrigerate the salad for about 30 minutes before serving to allow the flavors to meld.

Serve:
- Serve the Mediterranean Chickpea Salad as a refreshing side dish or a light main course.

This salad is not only delicious but also versatile. You can customize it by adding other Mediterranean ingredients like artichoke hearts, roasted red peppers, or cucumber.

Enjoy your vibrant and flavorful Mediterranean Chickpea Salad!

Easy Beef and Broccoli

Ingredients:

- 1 lb (450g) flank steak or sirloin, thinly sliced
- 1/2 cup low-sodium soy sauce
- 3 tablespoons oyster sauce
- 2 tablespoons brown sugar
- 2 tablespoons cornstarch
- 2 tablespoons vegetable oil (divided)
- 3 cups broccoli florets
- 3 cloves garlic, minced
- 1 teaspoon fresh ginger, grated
- Sesame seeds and green onions for garnish (optional)
- Cooked rice for serving

Instructions:

Marinate the Beef:
- In a bowl, combine the thinly sliced beef with soy sauce, oyster sauce, brown sugar, and cornstarch. Allow it to marinate for at least 15-20 minutes.

Cook the Broccoli:
- Steam or blanch the broccoli florets in boiling water for 2-3 minutes until they are bright green and slightly tender. Drain and set aside.

Sear the Beef:
- Heat 1 tablespoon of vegetable oil in a wok or large skillet over high heat.
- Add the marinated beef to the hot oil and sear for 2-3 minutes until it's browned and cooked through. Remove the beef from the wok and set it aside.

Sauté Garlic and Ginger:
- In the same wok, add another tablespoon of oil if needed. Sauté the minced garlic and grated ginger until fragrant.

Combine Beef and Broccoli:
- Add the cooked beef back to the wok along with the steamed broccoli. Toss everything together to combine and heat through.

Serve:
- Serve the Easy Beef and Broccoli over cooked rice.

- Garnish with sesame seeds and sliced green onions if desired.

This recipe is not only quick and easy but also versatile. Feel free to add other vegetables like bell peppers or carrots for extra color and nutrients. Enjoy your homemade Beef and Broccoli!

Caprese Sandwiches

Ingredients:

- Ciabatta bread or baguette, sliced
- Fresh tomatoes, sliced
- Fresh mozzarella cheese, sliced
- Fresh basil leaves
- Extra-virgin olive oil
- Balsamic glaze or balsamic reduction (optional)
- Salt and black pepper to taste

Instructions:

Prepare the Bread:
- Slice the ciabatta bread or baguette into individual sandwich-sized pieces.

Assemble the Sandwiches:
- Layer the slices of fresh tomatoes, mozzarella cheese, and fresh basil leaves on the bottom half of each bread slice.

Drizzle with Olive Oil:
- Drizzle extra-virgin olive oil over the tomato, mozzarella, and basil layers. This adds flavor and enhances the sandwich's moisture.

Season with Salt and Pepper:
- Sprinkle a pinch of salt and black pepper over the ingredients. Adjust according to your taste preferences.

Optional Balsamic Glaze:
- If desired, drizzle a small amount of balsamic glaze or balsamic reduction over the sandwich for a sweet and tangy kick.

Top with Second Bread Slice:
- Place the top half of the bread over the tomato, mozzarella, and basil layers to form a sandwich.

Serve:
- Serve the Caprese Sandwiches immediately.

These sandwiches are a wonderful embodiment of the fresh and vibrant flavors of the classic Caprese salad. They make for a light and satisfying lunch or picnic option. Enjoy!

Thai Basil Chicken Stir-Fry

Ingredients:

- 1 lb (450g) ground chicken
- 2 tablespoons vegetable oil
- 4 cloves garlic, minced
- 2 Thai bird chilies, finely chopped (adjust to spice preference)
- 1 cup fresh Thai basil leaves
- 1 red bell pepper, thinly sliced
- 1 green bell pepper, thinly sliced
- 1 onion, thinly sliced
- 3 tablespoons oyster sauce
- 1 tablespoon soy sauce
- 1 teaspoon fish sauce
- 1 teaspoon sugar
- Cooked jasmine rice, for serving

Instructions:

Prepare Ingredients:
- Mince the garlic, chop the Thai bird chilies, and slice the bell peppers and onion.

Cook Ground Chicken:
- Heat vegetable oil in a wok or large skillet over medium-high heat.
- Add minced garlic and chopped Thai bird chilies, and sauté for about 30 seconds until fragrant.
- Add ground chicken and cook, breaking it apart with a spoon, until it's no longer pink and starts to brown.

Add Vegetables:
- Add the sliced red and green bell peppers, and sliced onion to the wok. Stir-fry for 2-3 minutes until the vegetables are slightly tender but still crisp.

Make Sauce:
- In a small bowl, mix together oyster sauce, soy sauce, fish sauce, and sugar.

Add Sauce to Wok:

- Pour the sauce over the chicken and vegetables. Stir well to coat everything evenly.

Add Thai Basil:
- Once the vegetables are cooked to your liking and the sauce has coated the ingredients, add the fresh Thai basil leaves. Stir-fry for an additional 1-2 minutes until the basil is wilted.

Serve:
- Remove the wok from heat. Serve the Thai Basil Chicken Stir-Fry over cooked jasmine rice.

Optional Garnish:
- Garnish with additional fresh Thai basil leaves and sliced Thai bird chilies if you like it spicier.

Enjoy this Thai Basil Chicken Stir-Fry with its aromatic flavors and the perfect balance of sweet, savory, and spicy notes!

Margherita Pizza

Ingredients:

For the Pizza Dough:

- 2 1/4 teaspoons (1 packet) active dry yeast
- 1 teaspoon sugar
- 3/4 cup warm water (110°F/43°C)
- 2 cups all-purpose flour
- 1 teaspoon salt
- 1 tablespoon olive oil

For the Toppings:

- 1 cup pizza sauce (homemade or store-bought)
- 8 ounces fresh mozzarella cheese, sliced
- 2-3 large ripe tomatoes, thinly sliced
- Fresh basil leaves
- Extra-virgin olive oil
- Salt and black pepper to taste

Instructions:

Prepare the Pizza Dough:
- In a small bowl, combine the active dry yeast, sugar, and warm water. Let it sit for about 5-10 minutes until the mixture becomes frothy.
- In a large mixing bowl, combine the flour and salt. Make a well in the center and pour in the yeast mixture and olive oil.
- Mix until the dough comes together. Turn the dough onto a floured surface and knead for about 5 minutes until it becomes smooth and elastic.
- Place the dough in a lightly oiled bowl, cover with a damp cloth, and let it rise in a warm place for about 1-2 hours or until it doubles in size.

Preheat the Oven:
- Preheat your oven to the highest temperature it can go, typically around 500°F (260°C) or higher. If you have a pizza stone, place it in the oven during preheating.

Shape the Pizza:
- Punch down the risen dough and divide it into two portions for two pizzas.

- On a floured surface, roll out each portion into a thin round or oval shape.
- If using a pizza stone, transfer the rolled-out dough to a pizza peel or an inverted baking sheet dusted with cornmeal to prevent sticking.

Add Toppings:
- Spread a thin layer of pizza sauce over the dough, leaving a small border around the edges.
- Arrange slices of fresh mozzarella and tomato evenly over the sauce.
- Season with salt and black pepper to taste.

Bake the Pizza:
- If using a pizza stone, carefully transfer the pizza onto the preheated stone in the oven.
- Bake for about 10-12 minutes or until the crust is golden and the cheese is melted and bubbly.

Finish and Serve:
- Remove the pizza from the oven, sprinkle fresh basil leaves over the top, and drizzle with extra-virgin olive oil.
- Let the pizza cool for a few minutes before slicing.

Enjoy:
- Serve and enjoy your homemade Margherita Pizza!

This classic pizza is all about showcasing the quality of its ingredients. The simplicity of the Margherita Pizza allows the flavors of fresh tomatoes, mozzarella, and basil to shine.

Black Bean and Corn Quesadillas

Ingredients:

- 1 can (15 oz) black beans, drained and rinsed
- 1 cup frozen corn kernels, thawed
- 1 cup shredded cheddar cheese or Mexican blend cheese
- 1/2 cup diced red onion
- 1/4 cup chopped fresh cilantro
- 1 teaspoon ground cumin
- 1 teaspoon chili powder
- Salt and black pepper to taste
- 4 large flour tortillas
- Cooking spray or a bit of oil for cooking
- Guacamole, salsa, sour cream, or your favorite toppings for serving (optional)

Instructions:

Prepare the Filling:
- In a bowl, combine black beans, thawed corn, shredded cheese, diced red onion, chopped cilantro, ground cumin, chili powder, salt, and black pepper. Mix well to ensure even distribution of ingredients.

Assemble the Quesadillas:
- Lay out the flour tortillas on a clean surface.
- Spoon the black bean and corn mixture evenly onto one-half of each tortilla.

Fold and Seal:
- Fold the other half of the tortilla over the filling, creating a half-moon shape.
- Press down gently to seal the edges.

Cook the Quesadillas:
- Heat a large skillet or griddle over medium heat.
- Lightly coat the skillet with cooking spray or a bit of oil.
- Place the quesadillas in the skillet and cook for 3-4 minutes on each side or until golden brown and the cheese is melted.

Serve:
- Remove the quesadillas from the skillet and let them cool for a minute before slicing.

- Serve with guacamole, salsa, sour cream, or your favorite toppings if desired.

Enjoy:
- Enjoy your Black Bean and Corn Quesadillas as a tasty and satisfying meal!

Feel free to customize these quesadillas by adding ingredients like diced bell peppers, jalapeños, or your favorite cheese. They make for a quick and versatile dish that can be enjoyed for lunch, dinner, or even as a party appetizer.

Lemon Herb Grilled Chicken

Ingredients:

- 4 boneless, skinless chicken breasts
- 1/4 cup olive oil
- Zest and juice of 2 lemons
- 3 cloves garlic, minced
- 1 tablespoon fresh rosemary, chopped
- 1 tablespoon fresh thyme, chopped
- 1 teaspoon dried oregano
- Salt and black pepper to taste
- Lemon slices for garnish (optional)
- Fresh herbs for garnish (optional)

Instructions:

Prepare the Marinade:
- In a bowl, whisk together olive oil, lemon zest, lemon juice, minced garlic, chopped rosemary, chopped thyme, dried oregano, salt, and black pepper.

Marinate the Chicken:
- Place the chicken breasts in a shallow dish or a resealable plastic bag.
- Pour the marinade over the chicken, ensuring each piece is well-coated.
- Marinate in the refrigerator for at least 30 minutes to allow the flavors to infuse.

Preheat the Grill:
- Preheat your grill to medium-high heat.

Grill the Chicken:
- Remove the chicken from the marinade and let any excess drip off.
- Grill the chicken breasts for about 6-8 minutes per side or until they reach an internal temperature of 165°F (74°C) and have beautiful grill marks.

Rest the Chicken:
- Remove the chicken from the grill and let it rest for a few minutes before slicing. This helps retain the juices.

Garnish and Serve:
- Garnish the Lemon Herb Grilled Chicken with lemon slices and fresh herbs if desired.
- Serve with your favorite sides, such as grilled vegetables, salad, or rice.

Enjoy:

- Enjoy your flavorful and zesty Lemon Herb Grilled Chicken!

Feel free to customize the marinade with your favorite herbs and spices. This recipe is versatile and pairs well with a variety of side dishes, making it a great choice for a light and delicious meal.

Penne alla Vodka

Ingredients:

- 12 oz (340g) penne pasta
- 2 tablespoons olive oil
- 1 small onion, finely chopped
- 2 cloves garlic, minced
- 1/2 teaspoon red pepper flakes (optional, for heat)
- 1 cup tomato sauce
- 1/4 cup vodka
- 1/2 cup heavy cream
- Salt and black pepper to taste
- 1/4 cup grated Parmesan cheese
- Fresh basil or parsley for garnish

Instructions:

Cook the Pasta:
- Cook the penne pasta according to the package instructions in a large pot of salted boiling water until al dente. Reserve about 1/2 cup of pasta cooking water before draining.

Sauté Onions and Garlic:
- In a large skillet, heat olive oil over medium heat. Add finely chopped onions and sauté until they become translucent.
- Add minced garlic and red pepper flakes (if using) and cook for an additional 1-2 minutes until the garlic is fragrant.

Prepare the Sauce:
- Pour in the tomato sauce and vodka. Stir well and let it simmer for about 5 minutes to cook off the alcohol.
- Reduce the heat to low and add the heavy cream. Stir until the sauce is well combined and heated through.

Season and Finish:
- Season the sauce with salt and black pepper to taste. Adjust the seasoning according to your preference.
- Add the cooked and drained penne pasta to the sauce. Toss everything together until the pasta is well-coated in the creamy vodka sauce.

Add Parmesan and Garnish:

- Stir in the grated Parmesan cheese, allowing it to melt into the sauce and thicken it.
- Garnish with fresh basil or parsley.

Serve:
- Serve the Penne alla Vodka immediately, garnished with additional Parmesan if desired.

Enjoy this indulgent and flavorful pasta dish that combines the richness of the vodka-infused tomato sauce with the creamy texture of the heavy cream. It's a comforting and satisfying meal.

Teriyaki Tofu Stir-Fry

Ingredients:

- 1 block (14 oz) extra-firm tofu, pressed and cubed
- 2 tablespoons soy sauce
- 2 tablespoons teriyaki sauce
- 1 tablespoon sesame oil
- 2 tablespoons vegetable oil (for stir-frying)
- 1 bell pepper, thinly sliced
- 1 carrot, julienned
- 1 broccoli crown, cut into florets
- 3 green onions, sliced
- 2 cloves garlic, minced
- 1 tablespoon fresh ginger, grated
- Cooked rice or noodles for serving
- Sesame seeds and chopped green onions for garnish (optional)

Instructions:

Prepare the Tofu:
- Press the tofu to remove excess water. Cut it into cubes.

Marinate the Tofu:
- In a bowl, combine the cubed tofu with soy sauce, teriyaki sauce, and sesame oil. Let it marinate for at least 15-20 minutes.

Stir-Fry the Tofu:
- Heat 1 tablespoon of vegetable oil in a wok or large skillet over medium-high heat.
- Add the marinated tofu cubes and stir-fry until they are golden brown on all sides. Remove the tofu from the wok and set it aside.

Stir-Fry the Vegetables:
- In the same wok, add another tablespoon of vegetable oil.
- Add sliced bell pepper, julienned carrot, broccoli florets, green onions, minced garlic, and grated ginger.
- Stir-fry the vegetables for 4-5 minutes or until they are tender-crisp.

Combine Tofu and Vegetables:
- Return the cooked tofu to the wok with the stir-fried vegetables. Toss everything together until well combined.

Serve:

- Serve the Teriyaki Tofu Stir-Fry over cooked rice or noodles.
- Garnish with sesame seeds and chopped green onions if desired.

This Teriyaki Tofu Stir-Fry is a versatile dish, and you can customize it by adding your favorite vegetables or adjusting the level of sweetness in the teriyaki sauce. It's a quick and tasty vegetarian option for a weeknight dinner. Enjoy!

Greek Chicken Wraps

Ingredients:

For the Greek Chicken:

- 1 lb (450g) boneless, skinless chicken breasts, thinly sliced
- 2 tablespoons olive oil
- 1 teaspoon dried oregano
- 1 teaspoon dried thyme
- 1 teaspoon garlic powder
- Salt and black pepper to taste
- Juice of 1 lemon

For the Tzatziki Sauce:

- 1 cup Greek yogurt
- 1/2 cucumber, grated and drained
- 2 cloves garlic, minced
- 1 tablespoon fresh dill, chopped
- 1 tablespoon olive oil
- Salt and black pepper to taste

For the Wraps:

- Whole wheat or spinach tortillas
- Cherry tomatoes, halved
- Red onion, thinly sliced
- Feta cheese, crumbled
- Kalamata olives, sliced
- Fresh lettuce or spinach leaves

Instructions:

Marinate the Chicken:

- In a bowl, combine sliced chicken breasts with olive oil, dried oregano, dried thyme, garlic powder, salt, black pepper, and lemon juice. Let it marinate for at least 15 minutes.

Cook the Chicken:
- Heat a skillet over medium-high heat. Add the marinated chicken and cook for 5-6 minutes or until fully cooked and slightly browned. Set aside.

Prepare the Tzatziki Sauce:
- In a bowl, mix together Greek yogurt, grated and drained cucumber, minced garlic, chopped fresh dill, olive oil, salt, and black pepper. Stir well to combine.

Assemble the Wraps:
- Warm the tortillas according to the package instructions.
- Spread a generous spoonful of tzatziki sauce onto each tortilla.
- Add a portion of the cooked chicken to the center of each tortilla.
- Top with cherry tomatoes, red onion slices, crumbled feta cheese, Kalamata olives, and fresh lettuce or spinach leaves.

Wrap and Serve:
- Fold in the sides of the tortilla and then roll it up, creating a wrap.
- Serve the Greek Chicken Wraps immediately and enjoy!

These wraps are not only flavorful but also customizable. Feel free to add other Mediterranean-inspired ingredients like cucumber slices, roasted red peppers, or hummus. It's a perfect option for a light and satisfying meal.

Garlic Butter Shrimp Pasta

Ingredients:

- 8 oz (225g) linguine or your preferred pasta
- 1 lb (450g) large shrimp, peeled and deveined
- Salt and black pepper to taste
- 4 tablespoons unsalted butter, divided
- 4 cloves garlic, minced
- 1/2 teaspoon red pepper flakes (optional, for heat)
- 1 cup cherry tomatoes, halved
- 1/2 cup chicken broth
- Juice of 1 lemon
- 1/4 cup fresh parsley, chopped
- Grated Parmesan cheese for serving

Instructions:

Cook the Pasta:
- Cook the pasta according to package instructions in a large pot of salted boiling water until al dente. Reserve about 1/2 cup of pasta water before draining.

Season and Cook the Shrimp:
- Season the shrimp with salt and black pepper. In a large skillet, heat 2 tablespoons of butter over medium-high heat. Add the shrimp and cook for 1-2 minutes per side until they turn pink and opaque. Remove the shrimp from the skillet and set aside.

Make the Garlic Butter Sauce:
- In the same skillet, add the remaining 2 tablespoons of butter. Add minced garlic and red pepper flakes (if using) and sauté for about 1 minute until fragrant.
- Add the halved cherry tomatoes and cook for an additional 2 minutes until they start to soften.

Deglaze with Broth:
- Pour in the chicken broth to deglaze the skillet, scraping up any browned bits from the bottom.

Combine with Pasta and Shrimp:

- Return the cooked shrimp to the skillet. Add the cooked pasta, tossing everything together to coat in the garlic butter sauce.

Add Lemon and Parsley:
- Squeeze the juice of one lemon over the pasta and shrimp. Sprinkle fresh chopped parsley over the dish.

Adjust Consistency and Seasoning:
- If needed, add a bit of the reserved pasta cooking water to achieve your desired sauce consistency. Adjust the seasoning with more salt and black pepper if necessary.

Serve:
- Serve the Garlic Butter Shrimp Pasta immediately, garnished with grated Parmesan cheese if desired.

Enjoy your delicious Garlic Butter Shrimp Pasta!

Veggie Stir-Fry with Tofu

Ingredients:

- 1 block of firm or extra-firm tofu, pressed and cubed
- 2 tablespoons soy sauce
- 1 tablespoon sesame oil
- 1 tablespoon vegetable oil
- 1 onion, thinly sliced
- 2 bell peppers, thinly sliced (use a mix of colors for variety)
- 2 carrots, julienned
- 1 cup broccoli florets
- 1 cup snap peas, ends trimmed
- 3 cloves garlic, minced
- 1 tablespoon ginger, grated
- 2 tablespoons hoisin sauce
- 1 tablespoon rice vinegar
- 1 teaspoon Sriracha sauce (adjust to taste)
- 2 green onions, sliced (for garnish)
- Sesame seeds (for garnish)
- Cooked rice or noodles for serving

Instructions:

Prepare Tofu:
- Press the tofu to remove excess water by placing it between paper towels and placing a heavy object on top for about 15-20 minutes.
- Cut the pressed tofu into cubes and marinate them in soy sauce and sesame oil. Set aside for at least 15 minutes.

Stir-Fry:
- Heat vegetable oil in a large wok or skillet over medium-high heat.
- Add marinated tofu cubes and cook until golden brown on all sides. Remove tofu from the pan and set aside.

Vegetable Stir-Fry:
- In the same pan, add a bit more oil if needed.
- Stir-fry the sliced onions until translucent.
- Add bell peppers, carrots, broccoli, snap peas, minced garlic, and grated ginger. Stir-fry for 4-5 minutes until the vegetables are tender-crisp.

Sauce:
- In a small bowl, mix hoisin sauce, rice vinegar, and Sriracha sauce.
- Pour the sauce over the vegetables and stir to coat evenly.

Combine:
- Add the cooked tofu back into the pan and gently toss to combine with the vegetables and sauce.

Serve:
- Serve the veggie stir-fry with tofu over cooked rice or noodles.
- Garnish with sliced green onions and sesame seeds.

Enjoy your delicious and nutritious veggie stir-fry with tofu! Feel free to customize the vegetables and adjust the sauce according to your taste preferences.

Avocado and Black Bean Salad

Ingredients:

- 1 can (15 oz) black beans, drained and rinsed
- 2 ripe avocados, diced
- 1 cup corn kernels (fresh, canned, or frozen and thawed)
- 1 cup cherry tomatoes, halved
- 1/2 red onion, finely chopped
- 1/4 cup fresh cilantro, chopped
- Juice of 1-2 limes
- 2 tablespoons extra-virgin olive oil
- Salt and pepper to taste
- Optional: 1 jalapeño, finely chopped (for a bit of heat)

Instructions:

Prepare Ingredients:
- Rinse and drain the black beans.
- Dice the avocados and chop the red onion, cherry tomatoes, and cilantro.

Combine Ingredients:
- In a large mixing bowl, combine the black beans, diced avocados, corn, cherry tomatoes, chopped red onion, and cilantro.

Make the Dressing:
- In a small bowl, whisk together the lime juice, extra-virgin olive oil, salt, and pepper. If you like a bit of heat, you can add finely chopped jalapeño to the dressing.

Combine and Toss:
- Pour the dressing over the salad ingredients in the large mixing bowl.
- Gently toss the salad until all ingredients are well coated with the dressing.

Chill (Optional):
- You can refrigerate the salad for about 30 minutes to let the flavors meld together. This step is optional but can enhance the overall taste.

Serve:
- Serve the avocado and black bean salad as a side dish or a light main course.
- Garnish with additional cilantro or lime wedges if desired.

This salad is not only delicious but also versatile. You can customize it by adding ingredients like diced bell peppers, cucumber, or feta cheese. Enjoy this healthy and flavorful avocado and black bean salad!

Sweet and Sour Chicken

Ingredients:

For the Chicken:

- 1 lb (about 500g) boneless, skinless chicken breasts, cut into bite-sized pieces
- Salt and pepper to taste
- 1 cup cornstarch, for coating
- 2 eggs, beaten
- Vegetable oil for frying

For the Sweet and Sour Sauce:

- 1/2 cup ketchup
- 1/3 cup white vinegar
- 1/4 cup soy sauce
- 1 cup pineapple juice
- 3/4 cup granulated sugar
- 1 tablespoon cornstarch
- 1 red bell pepper, cut into chunks
- 1 green bell pepper, cut into chunks
- 1 cup pineapple chunks (fresh or canned)

For Garnish:

- Green onions, sliced
- Sesame seeds (optional)

Instructions:

Prepare the Chicken:
- Season the chicken pieces with salt and pepper.
- Place cornstarch in a shallow dish. Dip each chicken piece into beaten eggs, then coat with cornstarch, pressing lightly to adhere.

Fry the Chicken:
- In a large skillet or wok, heat vegetable oil over medium-high heat.

- Fry the coated chicken pieces until they are golden brown and cooked through. Remove and set aside on paper towels to drain excess oil.

Make the Sweet and Sour Sauce:
- In a bowl, whisk together ketchup, white vinegar, soy sauce, pineapple juice, sugar, and cornstarch until well combined.

Cook the Vegetables:
- In the same skillet or wok, stir-fry the bell peppers until slightly tender.
- Add the pineapple chunks and continue to stir-fry for another 1-2 minutes.

Combine and Simmer:
- Pour the sweet and sour sauce over the vegetables in the skillet. Stir to combine.
- Add the fried chicken back into the skillet, coating it with the sauce.
- Allow the mixture to simmer for a few minutes until the sauce thickens and the chicken is heated through.

Garnish and Serve:
- Garnish the sweet and sour chicken with sliced green onions and sesame seeds, if desired.
- Serve the dish over steamed rice or noodles.

Enjoy your homemade sweet and sour chicken with its delightful combination of flavors!

Pesto Chicken Panini

Ingredients:

- 4 boneless, skinless chicken breasts
- Salt and pepper to taste
- 1 cup basil pesto (store-bought or homemade)
- 8 slices of your favorite bread (ciabatta, sourdough, or whole grain work well)
- 8 slices of mozzarella or provolone cheese
- Olive oil or butter for grilling

Instructions:

Prepare the Chicken:
- Season the chicken breasts with salt and pepper.
- Cook the chicken breasts on a grill pan or in a skillet over medium-high heat until fully cooked, about 6-8 minutes per side. Make sure the internal temperature reaches 165°F (74°C).
- Once cooked, let the chicken rest for a few minutes before slicing it into thin strips.

Assemble the Panini:
- Lay out the slices of bread on a clean surface.
- Spread a generous amount of basil pesto on one side of each slice.
- Place a few slices of grilled chicken on half of the bread slices.
- Top the chicken with a slice of mozzarella or provolone cheese.
- Place the remaining slices of bread on top to form sandwiches, pesto side facing inwards.

Grill the Panini:
- Preheat a panini press or a grill pan over medium heat.
- Brush the outer sides of the sandwiches with olive oil or spread with softened butter.
- Place the sandwiches on the panini press or grill pan and cook until the bread is golden brown, and the cheese is melted (usually 3-5 minutes, depending on your equipment).

Serve:
- Once the Panini is grilled to your liking, remove it from the press or pan.
- Allow the Panini to cool for a minute before slicing it in half.
- Serve warm and enjoy your Pesto Chicken Panini!

Feel free to customize your Panini by adding other ingredients like roasted red peppers, sliced tomatoes, or fresh spinach for extra flavor and texture.

Quick Beef Burrito Bowls

Ingredients:

For the Beef:

- 1 lb ground beef
- 1 tablespoon olive oil
- 1 small onion, finely chopped
- 2 cloves garlic, minced
- 1 tablespoon taco seasoning
- Salt and pepper to taste

For the Burrito Bowls:

- Cooked rice (white or brown)
- Black beans, drained and rinsed
- Corn kernels (fresh, canned, or frozen and thawed)
- Cherry tomatoes, halved
- Avocado, sliced
- Shredded lettuce or spinach
- Shredded cheese (cheddar, Monterey Jack, or your preference)
- Salsa
- Sour cream
- Lime wedges for garnish

Instructions:

Cook the Beef:
- In a skillet, heat olive oil over medium-high heat.
- Add chopped onions and garlic, sautéing until softened.
- Add ground beef and cook until browned, breaking it apart with a spoon.
- Stir in taco seasoning, salt, and pepper. Cook for an additional 2-3 minutes until well combined.

Prepare the Burrito Bowls:
- In serving bowls, assemble the burrito bowls by placing a portion of cooked rice at the bottom.

Add Toppings:
- Top the rice with black beans, corn, cherry tomatoes, avocado slices, and shredded lettuce or spinach.

Add Seasoned Beef:
- Spoon the seasoned ground beef over the vegetable and rice mixture.

Top with Cheese and Condiments:
- Sprinkle shredded cheese on top and add salsa and sour cream as desired.

Garnish and Serve:
- Garnish the burrito bowls with lime wedges for a burst of citrus flavor.
- Serve immediately and enjoy your quick beef burrito bowls!

Feel free to customize your burrito bowls with additional toppings such as diced red onions, cilantro, jalapeños, or a drizzle of hot sauce based on your preferences. This versatile recipe allows you to create a delicious and well-balanced meal in no time.

Lemon Herb Salmon

Ingredients:

- 4 salmon fillets (about 6 ounces each), skin-on or skinless
- Salt and pepper to taste
- 2 tablespoons olive oil

For the Lemon Herb Marinade:

- Zest of 1 lemon
- Juice of 1 lemon
- 2 tablespoons fresh parsley, finely chopped
- 1 tablespoon fresh dill, finely chopped
- 2 cloves garlic, minced
- 2 tablespoons olive oil
- Salt and pepper to taste

Instructions:

Preheat the Oven:
- Preheat your oven to 400°F (200°C).

Prepare the Lemon Herb Marinade:
- In a small bowl, whisk together the lemon zest, lemon juice, chopped parsley, chopped dill, minced garlic, olive oil, salt, and pepper.

Marinate the Salmon:
- Place the salmon fillets in a shallow dish or a resealable plastic bag.
- Pour the lemon herb marinade over the salmon, making sure each fillet is well coated. Marinate for at least 15-30 minutes in the refrigerator.

Season with Salt and Pepper:
- Before cooking, season the salmon fillets with additional salt and pepper to taste.

Cook the Salmon:
- Heat olive oil in an oven-safe skillet over medium-high heat.
- Place the salmon fillets in the skillet, skin-side down if they have skin.
- Sear for 2-3 minutes until the bottom is golden brown.

Transfer to the Oven:

- If using an oven-safe skillet, transfer the entire skillet to the preheated oven. Otherwise, transfer the salmon to a baking dish.
- Bake for about 10-12 minutes or until the salmon is cooked through and flakes easily with a fork.

Serve:
- Remove the salmon from the oven and let it rest for a couple of minutes.
- Serve the lemon herb salmon fillets with your favorite side dishes.

Enjoy your Lemon Herb Salmon with its bright and herby flavors. It pairs well with roasted vegetables, quinoa, or a light salad.

Caprese Pasta Salad

Ingredients:

For the Salad:

- 8 oz (about 225g) fusilli or your favorite pasta
- 1 pint cherry tomatoes, halved
- 1 1/2 cups fresh mozzarella balls (bocconcini), halved
- 1/2 cup fresh basil leaves, torn
- Salt and black pepper to taste

For the Dressing:

- 1/4 cup extra-virgin olive oil
- 2 tablespoons balsamic vinegar
- 2 cloves garlic, minced
- Salt and black pepper to taste

Instructions:

Cook the Pasta:
- Cook the pasta according to the package instructions in a large pot of salted boiling water until al dente.
- Drain the pasta and rinse it under cold water to stop the cooking process. Allow it to cool completely.

Prepare the Dressing:
- In a small bowl, whisk together the olive oil, balsamic vinegar, minced garlic, salt, and pepper. Set aside.

Assemble the Salad:
- In a large bowl, combine the cooked and cooled pasta, cherry tomatoes, mozzarella balls, and torn basil leaves.

Add Dressing:
- Pour the dressing over the salad ingredients.

Toss and Season:
- Gently toss the salad until all the ingredients are well coated with the dressing.

- Season with additional salt and black pepper to taste.

Chill (Optional):
- Refrigerate the Caprese Pasta Salad for about 30 minutes to allow the flavors to meld. This step is optional but enhances the taste.

Serve:
- Serve the Caprese Pasta Salad as a refreshing side dish or a light main course.

Enjoy your delicious Caprese Pasta Salad with the delightful combination of fresh tomatoes, mozzarella, basil, and balsamic dressing! Feel free to customize it by adding ingredients like olives, pine nuts, or grilled chicken for additional flavor and texture.

Chicken and Vegetable Curry

Ingredients:

- 1.5 lbs (about 700g) boneless, skinless chicken thighs or breasts, cut into bite-sized pieces
- 2 tablespoons curry powder
- 1 teaspoon turmeric powder
- 1 teaspoon ground cumin
- 1 teaspoon ground coriander
- 1/2 teaspoon chili powder (adjust to taste)
- Salt and black pepper to taste
- 2 tablespoons vegetable oil
- 1 large onion, finely chopped
- 3 cloves garlic, minced
- 1 tablespoon fresh ginger, grated
- 1 can (14 oz) diced tomatoes
- 1 can (14 oz) coconut milk
- 2 cups mixed vegetables (e.g., carrots, bell peppers, peas, and potatoes), chopped
- Fresh cilantro for garnish
- Cooked rice or naan for serving

Instructions:

Marinate the Chicken:
- In a bowl, combine the chicken pieces with curry powder, turmeric, cumin, coriander, chili powder, salt, and black pepper. Allow it to marinate for at least 15-20 minutes.

Cook the Chicken:
- Heat vegetable oil in a large, deep skillet or pot over medium heat.
- Add the marinated chicken and cook until browned on all sides. Remove the chicken from the pan and set it aside.

Saute Aromatics:
- In the same pan, add a bit more oil if needed.
- Saute the chopped onion until softened, then add minced garlic and grated ginger. Cook for an additional 1-2 minutes until fragrant.

Simmer with Tomatoes and Coconut Milk:

- Add the diced tomatoes to the pan, scraping up any browned bits from the bottom.
- Pour in the coconut milk and bring the mixture to a simmer.

Add Chicken and Vegetables:
- Return the browned chicken to the pan.
- Add the mixed vegetables to the curry. Stir to combine.

Simmer and Cook:
- Cover the pan and let the curry simmer for about 20-25 minutes or until the chicken is cooked through, and the vegetables are tender.

Adjust Seasoning:
- Taste the curry and adjust the seasoning, adding more salt or spice if needed.

Serve:
- Serve the chicken and vegetable curry over cooked rice or with naan.
- Garnish with fresh cilantro.

Enjoy your homemade Chicken and Vegetable Curry! It's a comforting and flavorful dish that pairs well with rice or bread.

BBQ Turkey Burgers

Ingredients:

For the Turkey Burgers:

- 1.5 lbs ground turkey
- 1/2 cup breadcrumbs
- 1/4 cup red onion, finely chopped
- 2 cloves garlic, minced
- 1/4 cup barbecue sauce
- 1 teaspoon Worcestershire sauce
- 1 teaspoon dried oregano
- Salt and black pepper to taste
- Olive oil for brushing

For Serving:

- Burger buns
- Lettuce, tomato, red onion (sliced), and other preferred toppings
- Additional barbecue sauce for drizzling

Instructions:

Preheat Grill or Pan:
- Preheat your grill or a grill pan over medium-high heat.

Prepare Turkey Burger Mix:
- In a large bowl, combine ground turkey, breadcrumbs, chopped red onion, minced garlic, barbecue sauce, Worcestershire sauce, dried oregano, salt, and black pepper.
- Mix the ingredients until well combined. Be careful not to overmix to keep the burgers tender.

Shape Patties:
- Divide the turkey mixture into equal portions and shape them into burger patties.

Brush with Oil:

- Brush each side of the turkey patties lightly with olive oil. This helps prevent sticking and adds a nice sear when grilling.

Grill the Burgers:
- Place the turkey burgers on the preheated grill or grill pan.
- Grill for about 5-7 minutes per side, or until the internal temperature reaches 165°F (74°C) and the burgers are cooked through.

Toast the Buns:
- In the last few minutes of grilling, you can toast the burger buns on the grill until they are lightly golden.

Assemble and Serve:
- Place each grilled turkey burger on a bun.
- Add lettuce, tomato slices, red onion, or any other preferred toppings.
- Drizzle additional barbecue sauce over the top if desired.

Enjoy:
- Serve the BBQ Turkey Burgers immediately and enjoy with your favorite side dishes.

These BBQ Turkey Burgers are a tasty and healthier option, and you can customize them with your favorite toppings and condiments. They're perfect for a summer barbecue or a quick and satisfying weeknight dinner.

Shrimp Scampi with Linguine

Ingredients:

- 8 oz (about 225g) linguine pasta
- 1 lb large shrimp, peeled and deveined
- Salt and black pepper to taste
- 3 tablespoons olive oil
- 4 cloves garlic, minced
- 1/2 teaspoon red pepper flakes (optional, for some heat)
- 1/2 cup dry white wine
- Juice of 1 lemon
- Zest of 1 lemon
- 1/4 cup fresh parsley, chopped
- 3 tablespoons unsalted butter
- Grated Parmesan cheese for serving

Instructions:

Cook Linguine:
- Cook the linguine pasta in a large pot of salted boiling water according to the package instructions until al dente. Drain and set aside.

Prepare Shrimp:
- Pat the shrimp dry with paper towels and season them with salt and black pepper.

Sauté Shrimp:
- In a large skillet, heat olive oil over medium-high heat.
- Add the seasoned shrimp to the skillet and cook for 1-2 minutes per side until they turn pink and opaque. Remove the shrimp from the skillet and set aside.

Garlic and Red Pepper Flakes:
- In the same skillet, add minced garlic and red pepper flakes (if using). Sauté for about 30 seconds until the garlic becomes fragrant.

Deglaze with White Wine:
- Pour in the white wine to deglaze the pan, scraping up any browned bits from the bottom of the skillet.

Create Sauce:
- Add lemon juice, lemon zest, and chopped parsley to the skillet. Stir to combine.

- Reduce the heat to low and add the butter, allowing it to melt into the sauce.

Add Shrimp and Pasta:
- Return the cooked shrimp to the skillet and toss them in the sauce.
- Add the cooked linguine to the skillet, tossing everything together until the pasta is well coated with the sauce.

Serve:
- Divide the Shrimp Scampi and Linguine among plates.
- Garnish with additional chopped parsley and grated Parmesan cheese.

Enjoy your Shrimp Scampi with Linguine, a delightful combination of tender shrimp, aromatic garlic, and bright lemon flavors! It's a perfect dish for a special occasion or a quick and elegant weeknight dinner.

Veggie and Hummus Wraps

Ingredients:

- Whole-grain or spinach tortillas (number depends on servings)
- 1 cup hummus (store-bought or homemade)
- 2 cups mixed salad greens (e.g., spinach, arugula, or lettuce)
- 1 cucumber, thinly sliced
- 1 bell pepper (any color), thinly sliced
- 1 medium carrot, julienned or shredded
- 1 medium avocado, sliced
- Cherry tomatoes, halved
- Red onion, thinly sliced (optional)
- Feta cheese or goat cheese, crumbled (optional)
- Olive oil, balsamic vinegar, or your favorite dressing for drizzling
- Salt and pepper to taste

Instructions:

Prepare Vegetables:
- Wash and prepare all the vegetables as directed. You can use a variety of colorful veggies for a vibrant and nutritious wrap.

Warm Tortillas:
- If desired, warm the tortillas in a dry skillet for a few seconds on each side or according to the package instructions.

Spread Hummus:
- Spread a generous layer of hummus onto each tortilla, leaving about an inch from the edges.

Layer Vegetables:
- Layer the mixed salad greens, cucumber slices, bell pepper strips, julienned carrot, avocado slices, cherry tomatoes, and red onion (if using) on top of the hummus.

Optional Additions:
- Sprinkle crumbled feta cheese or goat cheese over the vegetables for added creaminess and flavor.

Season and Drizzle:
- Season the veggies with salt and pepper to taste.
- Drizzle olive oil, balsamic vinegar, or your favorite dressing over the vegetables for extra flavor.

Wrap and Serve:
- Fold the sides of the tortilla inwards, then roll it up tightly from the bottom to create a wrap.
- Repeat with the remaining tortillas.

Slice and Enjoy:
- If desired, slice the wraps in half diagonally.
- Serve immediately and enjoy your Veggie and Hummus Wraps!

These wraps are not only tasty but also customizable based on your preferences. Feel free to experiment with different vegetables, add a protein source like grilled chicken or tofu, and use your favorite hummus flavor for variety.

Spinach and Feta Stuffed Chicken Breasts

Ingredients:

- 4 boneless, skinless chicken breasts
- Salt and black pepper to taste
- 2 cups fresh spinach, chopped
- 1/2 cup feta cheese, crumbled
- 2 tablespoons olive oil
- 2 cloves garlic, minced
- 1 teaspoon dried oregano
- 1 teaspoon dried basil
- 1 teaspoon paprika
- Toothpicks or kitchen twine (to secure the stuffed chicken)

Instructions:

Preheat Oven:
- Preheat your oven to 375°F (190°C).

Prepare Chicken Breasts:
- Lay the chicken breasts flat on a cutting board. Using a sharp knife, make a horizontal slit along the thickest side of each chicken breast to create a pocket for stuffing. Be careful not to cut all the way through.

Season and Stuff:
- Season the inside of each chicken breast with salt and pepper.
- In a bowl, combine chopped spinach, crumbled feta, minced garlic, dried oregano, dried basil, and paprika. Mix well.
- Stuff each chicken breast with the spinach and feta mixture.

Secure with Toothpicks or Twine:
- Use toothpicks or kitchen twine to secure the open side of the chicken breasts, ensuring the stuffing stays inside.

Season the Outside:
- Brush the outside of the stuffed chicken breasts with olive oil and sprinkle with a bit of salt and pepper.

Sear the Chicken:
- Heat an oven-safe skillet over medium-high heat. Once hot, sear the stuffed chicken breasts on both sides until golden brown, about 2-3 minutes per side.

Bake in the Oven:
- Transfer the skillet to the preheated oven.
- Bake for about 20-25 minutes or until the chicken is cooked through, with an internal temperature of 165°F (74°C).

Rest and Serve:
- Remove the stuffed chicken breasts from the oven and let them rest for a few minutes before serving.
- Optionally, drizzle with any pan juices before serving.

Slice and Enjoy:
- Slice the stuffed chicken breasts into medallions and serve with your favorite side dishes.

These Spinach and Feta Stuffed Chicken Breasts are not only delicious but also make an impressive presentation. You can customize the stuffing with additional herbs, sun-dried tomatoes, or olives for extra flavor.

Easy Veggie Fried Rice

Ingredients:

- 2 cups cooked and chilled rice (preferably day-old rice)
- 2 tablespoons vegetable oil
- 1 cup mixed vegetables (carrots, peas, corn, bell peppers, and broccoli work well)
- 2 cloves garlic, minced
- 1 teaspoon ginger, minced
- 2 green onions, chopped
- 3 tablespoons soy sauce
- 1 tablespoon sesame oil (optional)
- 1/2 teaspoon salt (adjust to taste)
- 1/4 teaspoon black pepper
- 2 eggs, beaten (optional)

Instructions:

Prep Ingredients:
- If you haven't cooked the rice yet, cook it according to package instructions and let it cool in the refrigerator. Day-old rice works best for fried rice.
- Chop all the vegetables and set them aside.
- Mince the garlic and ginger, and chop the green onions.

Heat the Pan:
- Heat a large skillet or wok over medium-high heat.

Sauté Vegetables:
- Add vegetable oil to the hot pan.
- Add minced garlic and ginger, sauté for about 30 seconds until fragrant.
- Add mixed vegetables and stir-fry for 3-5 minutes until they are tender but still crisp.

Add Rice:
- Add the chilled cooked rice to the pan. Break up any clumps and stir-fry with the vegetables for a few minutes.

Seasoning:
- Pour soy sauce over the rice and vegetables. Add sesame oil if using.
- Sprinkle salt and black pepper, and toss everything together until well combined.

Optional: Add Eggs:
- Push the rice and vegetables to one side of the pan. Pour the beaten eggs into the empty side.
- Allow the eggs to cook for a moment, stirring occasionally, until scrambled.
- Mix the scrambled eggs with the rice and vegetables.

Finish and Garnish:
- Add chopped green onions and give everything a final toss.
- Taste and adjust seasoning if necessary.

Serve:
- Transfer the veggie fried rice to a serving dish and garnish with additional green onions if desired.

Enjoy your easy veggie fried rice! Feel free to customize the recipe by adding tofu, cashews, or your favorite protein for extra flavor and texture.

Chipotle Chicken Quesadillas

Ingredients:

- 2 cups cooked and shredded chicken (rotisserie chicken works well)
- 1 cup shredded cheese (cheddar, Monterey Jack, or a blend)
- 1/4 cup chopped fresh cilantro
- 1/4 cup diced red onion
- 1-2 chipotle peppers in adobo sauce, minced (adjust to taste)
- 1 teaspoon adobo sauce from the chipotle peppers
- 1 teaspoon ground cumin
- 1/2 teaspoon garlic powder
- Salt and pepper to taste
- 4 large flour tortillas
- 2 tablespoons vegetable oil or butter
- Sour cream, salsa, or guacamole for serving (optional)

Instructions:

Prepare the Chicken:
- Shred the cooked chicken and place it in a bowl.

Mix the Filling:
- Add shredded cheese, chopped cilantro, diced red onion, minced chipotle peppers, adobo sauce, ground cumin, garlic powder, salt, and pepper to the shredded chicken. Mix everything well.

Assemble the Quesadillas:
- Lay out the tortillas on a clean surface.
- Divide the chicken filling evenly among the tortillas, spreading it over half of each tortilla.

Fold and Cook:
- Fold the tortillas in half, covering the filling.
- Heat a large skillet or griddle over medium heat and add 1 tablespoon of vegetable oil or butter.
- Place the filled tortillas on the skillet and cook for 2-3 minutes on each side, or until the tortillas are golden brown and the cheese is melted.

Repeat:
- Repeat the process with the remaining quesadillas, adding more oil or butter to the skillet as needed.

Slice and Serve:
- Once the quesadillas are cooked, transfer them to a cutting board and let them rest for a minute.
- Slice each quesadilla into wedges and serve hot.

Optional: Serve with Sides:
- Serve the chipotle chicken quesadillas with sour cream, salsa, guacamole, or your favorite dipping sauce.

Enjoy your chipotle chicken quesadillas as a tasty and satisfying meal! Feel free to customize the filling with additional ingredients like diced tomatoes, black beans, or corn if you like.

Garlic Parmesan Zucchini Noodles

Ingredients:

- 4 medium-sized zucchini
- 2 tablespoons olive oil
- 4 cloves garlic, minced
- 1/4 teaspoon red pepper flakes (optional, for a bit of heat)
- Salt and black pepper to taste
- 1/2 cup grated Parmesan cheese
- 2 tablespoons chopped fresh parsley (optional, for garnish)

Instructions:

Prepare the Zucchini:
- Using a spiralizer or a julienne peeler, create zucchini noodles from the zucchinis. If you don't have a spiralizer, you can also use a knife to julienne the zucchini into thin strips.

Cook the Zucchini Noodles:
- Heat olive oil in a large skillet over medium heat.
- Add minced garlic and red pepper flakes (if using) to the skillet. Sauté for about 1-2 minutes until the garlic becomes fragrant.

Cook the Zoodles:
- Add the zucchini noodles to the skillet.
- Toss the zoodles in the garlic-infused oil, and cook for 2-3 minutes, stirring occasionally. Be careful not to overcook; you want the zucchini noodles to be tender but not mushy.

Season:
- Season the zoodles with salt and black pepper to taste. Remember that Parmesan cheese is salty, so adjust accordingly.

Add Parmesan:
- Sprinkle the grated Parmesan cheese over the zucchini noodles and toss until the cheese is melted and coats the zoodles evenly.

Garnish:
- If desired, garnish the garlic Parmesan zucchini noodles with chopped fresh parsley for a burst of color and freshness.

Serve:
- Transfer the zoodles to a serving dish and serve immediately.

Enjoy your garlic Parmesan zucchini noodles as a tasty, low-carb side dish or a light and satisfying main course. You can also customize this recipe by adding cherry tomatoes, spinach, or grilled chicken for extra flavor and nutrition.

Italian Sausage and Peppers Pasta

Ingredients:

- 8 ounces (about 225g) pasta of your choice (penne, rigatoni, or fusilli work well)
- 1 tablespoon olive oil
- 1 pound (about 450g) Italian sausage links, sweet or spicy, casings removed
- 1 onion, thinly sliced
- 1 red bell pepper, thinly sliced
- 1 yellow bell pepper, thinly sliced
- 3 cloves garlic, minced
- 1 teaspoon dried oregano
- 1 teaspoon dried basil
- 1/2 teaspoon red pepper flakes (optional, for some heat)
- Salt and black pepper to taste
- 1 can (14 ounces) crushed tomatoes
- 1/4 cup fresh basil, chopped (optional, for garnish)
- Grated Parmesan cheese for serving

Instructions:

Cook the Pasta:
- Cook the pasta according to package instructions in a large pot of salted boiling water until al dente. Drain and set aside.

Cook the Sausage:
- In a large skillet, heat olive oil over medium-high heat.
- Add the Italian sausage, breaking it up with a spoon as it cooks. Cook until browned and cooked through.

Add Vegetables:
- Add sliced onions and bell peppers to the skillet. Sauté until the vegetables are softened, about 5-7 minutes.

Add Garlic and Spices:
- Add minced garlic, dried oregano, dried basil, red pepper flakes (if using), salt, and black pepper to the skillet. Cook for an additional 1-2 minutes until the garlic becomes fragrant.

Combine with Crushed Tomatoes:
- Pour the crushed tomatoes into the skillet, stirring to combine. Simmer for about 10 minutes, allowing the flavors to meld.

Combine with Pasta:

- Add the cooked pasta to the skillet, tossing everything together until the pasta is well coated with the sausage and pepper mixture.

Adjust Seasoning:
- Taste and adjust the seasoning as needed. Add more salt, pepper, or red pepper flakes to suit your preferences.

Serve:
- Garnish with chopped fresh basil (if using) and serve hot. Optionally, sprinkle grated Parmesan cheese on top when serving.

Enjoy your Italian Sausage and Peppers Pasta, a delicious and satisfying meal that combines the flavors of Italian sausage, sweet bell peppers, and aromatic spices.

Mediterranean Quinoa Salad

Ingredients:

For the Salad:

- 1 cup quinoa, rinsed and cooked according to package instructions
- 1 cucumber, diced
- 1 cup cherry tomatoes, halved
- 1/2 cup Kalamata olives, pitted and sliced
- 1/2 cup red onion, finely chopped
- 1/2 cup feta cheese, crumbled
- 1/4 cup fresh parsley, chopped

For the Dressing:

- 1/4 cup extra-virgin olive oil
- 2 tablespoons red wine vinegar
- 1 clove garlic, minced
- 1 teaspoon dried oregano
- Salt and black pepper to taste

Instructions:

Cook Quinoa:
- Rinse the quinoa under cold water and cook it according to the package instructions. Once cooked, let it cool to room temperature.

Prepare Vegetables:
- In a large mixing bowl, combine the diced cucumber, cherry tomatoes, Kalamata olives, chopped red onion, crumbled feta cheese, and chopped fresh parsley.

Make the Dressing:
- In a small bowl, whisk together the extra-virgin olive oil, red wine vinegar, minced garlic, dried oregano, salt, and black pepper. Adjust the seasoning to taste.

Combine Salad and Dressing:
- Add the cooked and cooled quinoa to the bowl of vegetables.
- Pour the dressing over the salad ingredients.

Toss and Chill:

- Gently toss all the ingredients together until well combined and evenly coated with the dressing.
- Cover the bowl and refrigerate the salad for at least 30 minutes to allow the flavors to meld.

Serve:
- Before serving, give the salad a final toss.
- Garnish with additional fresh parsley and crumbled feta if desired.

Optional Additions:
- You can add other Mediterranean ingredients like artichoke hearts, roasted red peppers, or pine nuts for extra flavor and texture.

Enjoy your Mediterranean Quinoa Salad as a light and wholesome meal or a delightful side dish. It's perfect for picnics, potlucks, or as a refreshing option on a warm day.

Quick Margherita Flatbread

Ingredients:

- 1 flatbread (store-bought or homemade)
- 2 tablespoons olive oil
- 2 cloves garlic, minced
- 1 cup fresh mozzarella, sliced or torn into pieces
- 1 cup cherry tomatoes, halved
- Fresh basil leaves
- Salt and black pepper to taste
- Balsamic glaze (optional, for drizzling)

Instructions:

Preheat the Oven:
- Preheat your oven to 400°F (200°C).

Prepare the Flatbread:
- Place the flatbread on a baking sheet or pizza stone.

Garlic Infused Olive Oil:
- In a small bowl, mix the minced garlic with olive oil.

Brush the Flatbread:
- Brush the flatbread with the garlic-infused olive oil, covering the entire surface.

Add Mozzarella:
- Distribute the fresh mozzarella evenly over the flatbread.

Add Cherry Tomatoes:
- Place the halved cherry tomatoes on top of the mozzarella.

Season:
- Season with salt and black pepper to taste.

Bake:
- Bake in the preheated oven for about 10-12 minutes or until the cheese is melted, and the edges of the flatbread are golden brown.

Add Fresh Basil:
- Once out of the oven, scatter fresh basil leaves over the hot flatbread.

Optional: Drizzle with Balsamic Glaze:
- For an extra burst of flavor, drizzle the Margherita flatbread with balsamic glaze.

Slice and Serve:

- Slice the flatbread into desired portions and serve immediately.

Enjoy your quick Margherita flatbread as a simple and satisfying meal or as an appetizer. The combination of fresh mozzarella, juicy cherry tomatoes, and fragrant basil makes for a delightful and timeless flavor.

Chicken Caesar Wraps

Ingredients:

For the Caesar Dressing:

- 1/2 cup mayonnaise
- 2 tablespoons grated Parmesan cheese
- 1 tablespoon Dijon mustard
- 2 cloves garlic, minced
- 1 tablespoon fresh lemon juice
- Salt and black pepper to taste

For the Chicken:

- 1 pound (about 450g) boneless, skinless chicken breasts
- 1 tablespoon olive oil
- Salt and black pepper to taste
- 1 teaspoon dried oregano
- 1 teaspoon garlic powder

For the Wraps:

- Large flour tortillas
- Romaine lettuce, chopped
- Croutons
- Additional Parmesan cheese, grated
- Cherry tomatoes, halved (optional)

Instructions:

Prepare the Caesar Dressing:
- In a bowl, whisk together mayonnaise, grated Parmesan cheese, Dijon mustard, minced garlic, lemon juice, salt, and black pepper. Set aside.

Cook the Chicken:
- Season the chicken breasts with salt, black pepper, dried oregano, and garlic powder.

- In a skillet over medium heat, heat olive oil. Add the chicken breasts and cook until fully cooked, about 5-7 minutes per side, depending on thickness. Once cooked, let them rest for a few minutes, then slice them into strips.

Assemble the Wraps:
- Lay out the flour tortillas on a clean surface.
- Spread a generous spoonful of the Caesar dressing onto each tortilla.

Add Chicken and Vegetables:
- Place sliced chicken strips on top of the dressing.
- Add chopped Romaine lettuce, croutons, and additional Parmesan cheese.

Optional: Add Cherry Tomatoes:
- If desired, add halved cherry tomatoes for extra freshness.

Wrap and Serve:
- Fold the sides of the tortilla in, and then roll it up tightly to create the wrap.

Slice and Enjoy:
- Slice the wraps in half diagonally and serve immediately.

These Chicken Caesar wraps are a perfect combination of crisp lettuce, tender chicken, and flavorful Caesar dressing. They make a great lunch or dinner option, and you can customize them with your favorite additions like bacon, avocado, or extra veggies.

Teriyaki Vegetable Stir-Fry

Ingredients:

For the Teriyaki Sauce:

- 1/4 cup soy sauce
- 2 tablespoons mirin (sweet rice wine)
- 1 tablespoon rice vinegar
- 2 tablespoons brown sugar
- 1 teaspoon sesame oil
- 1 teaspoon grated ginger
- 2 cloves garlic, minced
- 1 tablespoon cornstarch (optional, for thickening)

For the Stir-Fry:

- 2 tablespoons vegetable oil
- 1 pound (about 450g) mixed vegetables (broccoli, bell peppers, carrots, snap peas, etc.), sliced or chopped
- 1 cup firm tofu or chicken, cubed (optional)
- Cooked rice or noodles for serving
- Sesame seeds and chopped green onions for garnish

Instructions:

Prepare the Teriyaki Sauce:
- In a small bowl, whisk together soy sauce, mirin, rice vinegar, brown sugar, sesame oil, grated ginger, and minced garlic. If you prefer a thicker sauce, mix in cornstarch as well.

Prepare the Stir-Fry Ingredients:
- If using tofu, press and cube it. If using chicken, cut it into bite-sized pieces. Prepare the vegetables by washing and chopping them.

Cook Tofu or Chicken (Optional):
- If using tofu, heat 1 tablespoon of vegetable oil in a large skillet or wok over medium heat. Add cubed tofu and cook until golden brown on all sides. Remove from the pan and set aside.
- If using chicken, cook it in the same pan until browned and cooked through. Remove and set aside.

Cook the Vegetables:
- In the same pan, add another tablespoon of vegetable oil.
- Add the mixed vegetables to the pan and stir-fry for 3-5 minutes until they are crisp-tender.

Combine Tofu/Chicken and Sauce:
- If using tofu or chicken, add it back to the pan with the vegetables.
- Pour the teriyaki sauce over the tofu/chicken and vegetables. Stir well to coat everything evenly.

Simmer and Thicken (Optional):
- Allow the mixture to simmer for a couple of minutes, allowing the sauce to thicken. If you used cornstarch, this will help in the thickening process.

Serve:
- Serve the teriyaki vegetable stir-fry over cooked rice or noodles.
- Garnish with sesame seeds and chopped green onions.

Enjoy your homemade teriyaki vegetable stir-fry, a tasty and nutritious meal that's sure to satisfy your cravings for flavorful Asian-inspired cuisine.

Pesto Shrimp and Tomato Pasta

Ingredients:

- 8 ounces (about 225g) linguine or your favorite pasta
- 1 pound (about 450g) large shrimp, peeled and deveined
- Salt and black pepper to taste
- 2 tablespoons olive oil
- 3 cloves garlic, minced
- 1 pint (about 2 cups) cherry tomatoes, halved
- 1/2 cup homemade or store-bought pesto
- 1/4 cup grated Parmesan cheese
- Fresh basil leaves for garnish

Instructions:

Cook the Pasta:
- Cook the pasta according to package instructions in a large pot of salted boiling water until al dente. Drain and set aside.

Season and Cook the Shrimp:
- Season the shrimp with salt and black pepper.
- In a large skillet, heat olive oil over medium-high heat. Add the minced garlic and cook for about 30 seconds until fragrant.
- Add the seasoned shrimp to the skillet and cook for 2-3 minutes per side, or until they are opaque and cooked through. Remove the shrimp from the pan and set aside.

Sauté Tomatoes:
- In the same skillet, add the halved cherry tomatoes. Sauté for 2-3 minutes until they start to soften and release their juices.

Combine with Pesto:
- Add the cooked pasta to the skillet with the tomatoes.
- Stir in the pesto, ensuring that the pasta and tomatoes are well-coated.

Add Shrimp and Parmesan:
- Gently fold in the cooked shrimp and grated Parmesan cheese. Toss everything together until the shrimp, pasta, and tomatoes are evenly mixed.

Adjust Seasoning:
- Taste and adjust the seasoning with additional salt and black pepper if needed.

Garnish and Serve:
- Garnish the pesto shrimp and tomato pasta with fresh basil leaves.
- Serve hot, and optionally, sprinkle extra Parmesan cheese on top when serving.

Enjoy your delicious and flavorful pesto shrimp and tomato pasta. It's a perfect combination of vibrant colors and tastes, making it a great option for a quick and satisfying meal.

BBQ Pulled Chicken Sandwiches

Ingredients:

For the Pulled Chicken:

- 1.5 to 2 pounds (about 680 to 907g) boneless, skinless chicken breasts or thighs
- Salt and black pepper to taste
- 1 teaspoon garlic powder
- 1 teaspoon onion powder
- 1 teaspoon smoked paprika
- 1 cup barbecue sauce (homemade or store-bought)
- 1/2 cup chicken broth or water

For the Sandwiches:

- Hamburger buns
- Coleslaw (optional, for topping)
- Pickles (optional, for serving)

Instructions:

Season the Chicken:
- Season the chicken breasts or thighs with salt, black pepper, garlic powder, onion powder, and smoked paprika.

Cook the Chicken:
- In a slow cooker or Instant Pot, place the seasoned chicken. Pour barbecue sauce and chicken broth (or water) over the chicken.
- For a slow cooker: Cook on low for 6-8 hours or on high for 3-4 hours until the chicken is tender and easily shreds.
- For an Instant Pot: Cook on the "Poultry" setting for about 15-20 minutes, followed by a natural release or quick release depending on your preference.
- If cooking on the stove, place the seasoned chicken in a large pot with barbecue sauce and chicken broth. Simmer on low heat for 45-60 minutes or until the chicken is tender and can be easily shredded.

Shred the Chicken:

- Once cooked, shred the chicken using two forks or a stand mixer. If using a stand mixer, place the cooked chicken in the mixer bowl, use the paddle attachment, and mix on low speed until shredded.

Combine with BBQ Sauce:
- Mix the shredded chicken with additional barbecue sauce, if desired, for extra flavor and moisture.

Assemble the Sandwiches:
- Toast the hamburger buns if you like.
- Place a generous portion of pulled chicken on the bottom half of each bun.

Optional Toppings:
- Top the pulled chicken with coleslaw for a crunchy, refreshing contrast. Add pickles if desired.

Serve:
- Cap the sandwiches with the other half of the buns and serve immediately.

Enjoy your BBQ pulled chicken sandwiches, a delicious and comforting meal that's perfect for casual gatherings or weeknight dinners.

Szechuan Tofu and Vegetable Stir-Fry

Ingredients:

For the Sauce:

- 3 tablespoons soy sauce
- 2 tablespoons rice vinegar
- 1 tablespoon hoisin sauce
- 1 tablespoon Szechuan sauce or chili garlic sauce (adjust to taste)
- 1 tablespoon cornstarch
- 1 tablespoon water

For the Stir-Fry:

- 14 ounces (about 400g) firm tofu, pressed and cubed
- 2 tablespoons vegetable oil
- 3 cloves garlic, minced
- 1 tablespoon ginger, minced
- 1 red bell pepper, thinly sliced
- 1 yellow bell pepper, thinly sliced
- 1 carrot, julienned
- 1 cup broccoli florets
- 1 cup snap peas, trimmed
- 2 green onions, sliced (for garnish)
- Sesame seeds (for garnish)
- Cooked rice or noodles for serving

Instructions:

Prepare the Sauce:
- In a small bowl, whisk together soy sauce, rice vinegar, hoisin sauce, Szechuan sauce (or chili garlic sauce), cornstarch, and water. Set aside.

Prepare the Tofu:
- Press the tofu to remove excess water. Cut the pressed tofu into cubes.

Stir-Fry the Tofu:

- In a large skillet or wok, heat 1 tablespoon of vegetable oil over medium-high heat.
- Add the tofu cubes and stir-fry until golden brown on all sides. Remove tofu from the pan and set aside.

Cook the Vegetables:
- In the same pan, add another tablespoon of vegetable oil.
- Add minced garlic and ginger, stir-frying for about 30 seconds until fragrant.
- Add the sliced red and yellow bell peppers, julienned carrots, broccoli florets, and snap peas. Stir-fry for 3-5 minutes until the vegetables are crisp-tender.

Combine Tofu and Sauce:
- Add the cooked tofu back to the pan with the vegetables.
- Pour the prepared sauce over the tofu and vegetables. Stir well to coat everything evenly.

Simmer and Thicken:
- Allow the mixture to simmer for a couple of minutes until the sauce thickens.

Garnish and Serve:
- Garnish the stir-fry with sliced green onions and sesame seeds.
- Serve over cooked rice or noodles.

Enjoy your Szechuan Tofu and Vegetable Stir-Fry, a delicious and spicy dish with a perfect balance of flavors and textures! Adjust the spice level according to your preference by varying the amount of Szechuan sauce or chili garlic sauce.

Caprese Chicken Skillet

Ingredients:

- 4 boneless, skinless chicken breasts
- Salt and black pepper to taste
- 1 tablespoon olive oil
- 2 teaspoons Italian seasoning (or a mixture of dried basil, oregano, and thyme)
- 2 cups cherry tomatoes, halved
- 8 ounces fresh mozzarella cheese, sliced
- Balsamic glaze (for drizzling, optional)
- Fresh basil leaves (for garnish)

Instructions:

Preheat the Oven:
- Preheat your oven to 400°F (200°C).

Season the Chicken:
- Season the chicken breasts with salt, black pepper, and Italian seasoning on both sides.

Sear the Chicken:
- In an oven-safe skillet, heat olive oil over medium-high heat.
- Sear the chicken breasts for 2-3 minutes on each side, or until they develop a golden-brown crust.

Add Tomatoes:
- Add the halved cherry tomatoes to the skillet, placing them around the seared chicken.

Bake:
- Transfer the skillet to the preheated oven and bake for 20-25 minutes or until the chicken is cooked through (internal temperature of 165°F or 74°C).

Add Mozzarella:
- Remove the skillet from the oven and place slices of fresh mozzarella over each chicken breast.

Broil:
- Set your oven to broil and return the skillet to the oven for 2-3 minutes or until the cheese is melted and bubbly.

Drizzle with Balsamic Glaze (Optional):

- Drizzle balsamic glaze over the chicken and tomatoes for added flavor. If you don't have balsamic glaze, you can reduce balsamic vinegar on the stovetop until it thickens.

Garnish and Serve:
- Garnish the Caprese Chicken Skillet with fresh basil leaves.

Serve:
- Serve the chicken breasts over a bed of greens, pasta, or alongside your favorite side dish.

Enjoy your Caprese Chicken Skillet, a delicious and visually appealing dish that brings together the flavors of juicy tomatoes, fresh mozzarella, and fragrant basil with perfectly cooked chicken.

Turkey and Avocado Wrap

Ingredients:

- 4 large whole wheat or spinach tortillas
- 1 pound (about 450g) sliced turkey breast
- 2 avocados, sliced
- 1 cup cherry tomatoes, halved
- 1 cup lettuce or spinach leaves
- 1/2 cup red onion, thinly sliced
- 1/2 cup shredded cheese (cheddar, Monterey Jack, or your choice)
- 1/4 cup mayonnaise or Greek yogurt
- 2 tablespoons Dijon mustard
- Salt and black pepper to taste

Instructions:

Prepare the Sauce:
- In a small bowl, mix together mayonnaise (or Greek yogurt) and Dijon mustard. Season with salt and black pepper to taste. This will be the spread for your wraps.

Assemble the Wraps:
- Lay out the tortillas on a clean surface.

Spread the Sauce:
- Spread the mayo-Dijon mixture evenly over each tortilla.

Layer Ingredients:
- On each tortilla, place a layer of sliced turkey, avocado slices, cherry tomatoes, lettuce or spinach leaves, red onion, and shredded cheese.

Fold and Roll:
- Fold in the sides of the tortilla and then roll it up tightly, creating a wrap.

Slice if Desired:
- If you prefer, slice the wraps in half diagonally for easier handling.

Serve:
- Serve the Turkey and Avocado Wraps immediately, or you can wrap them in parchment paper or foil for an on-the-go meal.

Enjoy your Turkey and Avocado Wraps, a delicious and balanced combination of protein, veggies, and healthy fats. Feel free to customize the wraps with additional ingredients like bacon, sprouts, or your favorite dressing for added flavor.

Lemon Garlic Shrimp Scampi

Ingredients:

- 8 ounces (about 225g) linguine or spaghetti
- 1 pound (about 450g) large shrimp, peeled and deveined
- Salt and black pepper to taste
- 3 tablespoons olive oil
- 4 cloves garlic, minced
- 1/2 teaspoon red pepper flakes (optional, for some heat)
- 1/2 cup chicken broth
- Zest and juice of 1 lemon
- 1/4 cup dry white wine (optional)
- 1/4 cup chopped fresh parsley
- Grated Parmesan cheese (for serving)
- Lemon wedges (for serving)

Instructions:

Cook the Pasta:
- Cook the pasta according to package instructions in a large pot of salted boiling water until al dente. Drain and set aside.

Season and Cook the Shrimp:
- Season the shrimp with salt and black pepper.
- In a large skillet, heat 2 tablespoons of olive oil over medium-high heat. Add the shrimp and cook for 2-3 minutes per side until they are opaque and cooked through. Remove the shrimp from the pan and set aside.

Make the Sauce:
- In the same skillet, add the remaining 1 tablespoon of olive oil.
- Add minced garlic and red pepper flakes (if using) to the skillet. Sauté for about 30 seconds until fragrant.
- Pour in the chicken broth, white wine (if using), lemon zest, and lemon juice. Bring the mixture to a simmer.

Combine with Shrimp and Pasta:
- Add the cooked shrimp and drained pasta to the skillet. Toss everything together until well coated with the lemon garlic sauce.

Finish and Garnish:
- Sprinkle chopped fresh parsley over the shrimp and pasta. Toss again to combine.

Serve:
- Serve the Lemon Garlic Shrimp Scampi hot, garnished with grated Parmesan cheese and lemon wedges on the side.

Enjoy your flavorful and zesty Lemon Garlic Shrimp Scampi. This dish is perfect for a quick and impressive weeknight dinner or a special occasion.

Cilantro Lime Chicken Tacos

Ingredients:

For the Cilantro Lime Chicken:

- 1 pound (about 450g) boneless, skinless chicken breasts
- Salt and black pepper to taste
- 1 teaspoon ground cumin
- 1 teaspoon paprika
- 1 teaspoon garlic powder
- Zest and juice of 2 limes
- 2 tablespoons chopped fresh cilantro
- 2 tablespoons olive oil

For the Tacos:

- 8 small flour or corn tortillas
- 1 cup shredded lettuce
- 1 cup diced tomatoes
- 1/2 cup diced red onion
- 1/2 cup chopped fresh cilantro
- Lime wedges for serving
- Sour cream or Greek yogurt (optional)

Instructions:

Marinate the Chicken:
- In a bowl, combine the chicken breasts with salt, black pepper, ground cumin, paprika, garlic powder, lime zest, lime juice, chopped cilantro, and olive oil. Allow it to marinate for at least 15-20 minutes.

Cook the Chicken:
- Preheat a grill or grill pan over medium-high heat.
- Grill the marinated chicken for about 6-8 minutes per side, or until fully cooked and nicely charred. Alternatively, you can use a skillet on the stovetop.

Rest and Slice:

- Let the chicken rest for a few minutes before slicing it into thin strips.

Prepare Taco Ingredients:
- Warm the tortillas according to package instructions.
- Assemble your taco toppings, including shredded lettuce, diced tomatoes, diced red onion, and chopped cilantro.

Assemble Tacos:
- Fill each tortilla with sliced cilantro lime chicken and your desired toppings.

Serve:
- Serve the Cilantro Lime Chicken Tacos with lime wedges on the side for squeezing over the tacos.
- Optionally, add a dollop of sour cream or Greek yogurt.

Enjoy your Cilantro Lime Chicken Tacos – a delicious and vibrant dish that's perfect for a quick and satisfying meal. Feel free to customize the toppings to suit your preferences!

Broccoli Cheddar Stuffed Chicken

Ingredients:

- 4 boneless, skinless chicken breasts
- Salt and black pepper to taste
- 1 cup cooked and chopped broccoli
- 1 cup shredded cheddar cheese
- 1/2 cup mayonnaise
- 1 clove garlic, minced
- 1 teaspoon Dijon mustard
- 1 cup breadcrumbs (for coating)
- 2 tablespoons olive oil

Instructions:

Preheat the Oven:
- Preheat your oven to 375°F (190°C).

Prepare the Chicken:
- Lay out the chicken breasts on a clean surface. Season both sides with salt and black pepper.

Make the Filling:
- In a bowl, combine the chopped broccoli, shredded cheddar cheese, mayonnaise, minced garlic, and Dijon mustard. Mix well until all the ingredients are evenly incorporated.

Create a Pocket:
- Carefully cut a slit horizontally into the thickest part of each chicken breast to create a pocket. Be careful not to cut all the way through.

Stuff the Chicken:
- Stuff each chicken breast pocket with the broccoli and cheddar mixture, pressing it down gently.

Secure with Toothpicks:
- If needed, secure the openings with toothpicks to keep the stuffing in place.

Coat with Breadcrumbs:
- Roll each stuffed chicken breast in breadcrumbs to coat the outside evenly.

Sear the Chicken:

- In an oven-safe skillet, heat olive oil over medium-high heat. Sear the stuffed chicken breasts for 2-3 minutes on each side until they develop a golden-brown crust.

Finish in the Oven:
- Transfer the skillet to the preheated oven and bake for 20-25 minutes or until the chicken is cooked through and the cheese is melted and bubbly.

Serve:
- Allow the Broccoli Cheddar Stuffed Chicken to rest for a few minutes before serving.
- Remove any toothpicks before serving.

Enjoy your Broccoli Cheddar Stuffed Chicken, a hearty and flavorful dish that's sure to impress. Serve it with your favorite side dishes, such as roasted vegetables, rice, or mashed potatoes.

www.ingramcontent.com/pod-product-compliance
Lightning Source LLC
LaVergne TN
LVHW081605060526
838201LV00054B/2086